First Guide to Maps

Mapping Your Community

Marta Segal Block and
Daniel R. Block

Heinemann
LIBRARY

www.heinemann.co.uk/library
Visit our website to find out more information about Heinemann Library books.

To order:
☎ Phone 44 (0) 1865 888066
▤ Send a fax to 44 (0) 1865 314091
💻 Visit the Heinemann Bookshop at www.heinemann.co.uk/library to browse our catalogue and order online.

First published in Great Britain by Heinemann Library, Halley Court, Jordan Hill, Oxford OX2 8EJ, part of Pearson Education. Heinemann is a registered trademark of Pearson Education Ltd.

Editorial: Cassie Mayer and Sian Smith
Design: Jennifer Lacki, Kimberly R. Miracle, and Betsy Wernert
Production: Duncan Gilbert

Illustrated by Mapping specialists
Originated by Modern Age
Printed and bound in China by South China Printing Co. Ltd

ISBN: 978 0 431 12784 2
12 11 10 09 08
10 9 8 7 6 5 4 3 2 1

British Library Cataloguing in Publication Data
Block, Marta Segal

Mapping your community. - (First guide to maps)
1. Maps - Juvenile literature 2. Map scales - Juvenile literature 3. Cartography - Juvenile literature 4. Human settlements - Juvenile literature
I. Title II. Block, Daniel, 1967-
912

Acknowledgements
The author and publishers are grateful to the following for permission to reproduce copyright material: ©age footstock p. **26** (Jeff Greenberg); Alamy p. **18** (Dennis MacDonald); Corbis p. **17** (Will & Deni McIntyre); drr. net p. **27** (Dino Fracchia); Getty Images pp. **6** (Royalty Free), **7** (Panoramic Images); Map Resources p. **4**; www. jasonhawkes.com p. **5**.

Cover image reproduced with permission of www. jasonhawkes.com.

Every effort has been made to contact copyright holders of any material reproduced in this book. Any omissions will be rectified in subsequent printings if notice is given to the publishers.

Contents

Any words appearing in the text in bold, **like this**, are explained in the glossary.

What are maps?

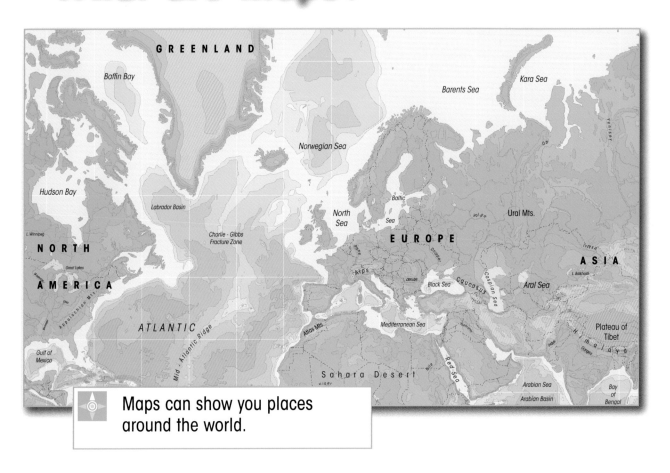

Maps can show you places around the world.

A map is a flat drawing of a part of the world. People who make maps are called **cartographers**.

You can use maps to learn about places far from where you live. You can also use them to learn about places close by.

Maps show places from a bird's eye view.

Mapping your community

A community is a group of people who have something in common. A community is a place where people might live, work, and play. There are big communities and small communities.

Your classroom and all the people in it are one community.

A city is a large community.

Your neighbourhood is a small community. A town
or city is a bigger community. It is part of an even
larger community, the country. Each community needs
many maps.

Reading maps

Maps have many features that help you to read them.

Map title

Most maps have a **title**. A map title tells you what information is on the map. For example, a map of a small town may list the town's name as the map title.

Compass rose

Many maps have a **compass rose**. This feature shows the **cardinal directions**. The cardinal directions are north, south, east, and west. North often points towards the top of the map.

Milton town centre

Map symbols

Maps have many **symbols**. Symbols are small shapes and signs that represent objects in real life. For example, dots on a map may show cities. A star may show the **capital** of a country. The capital is the place where leaders of a country meet and work.

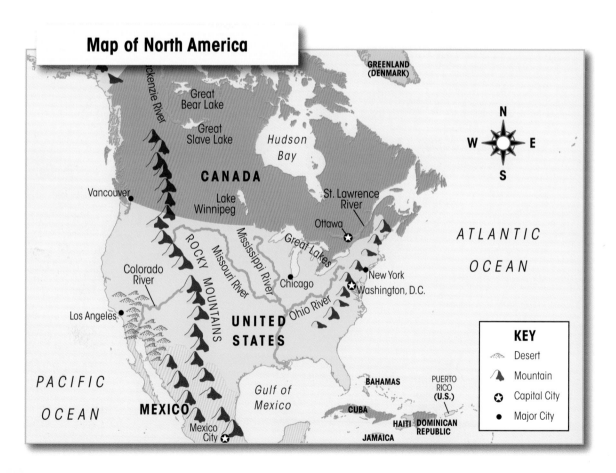

Map of North America

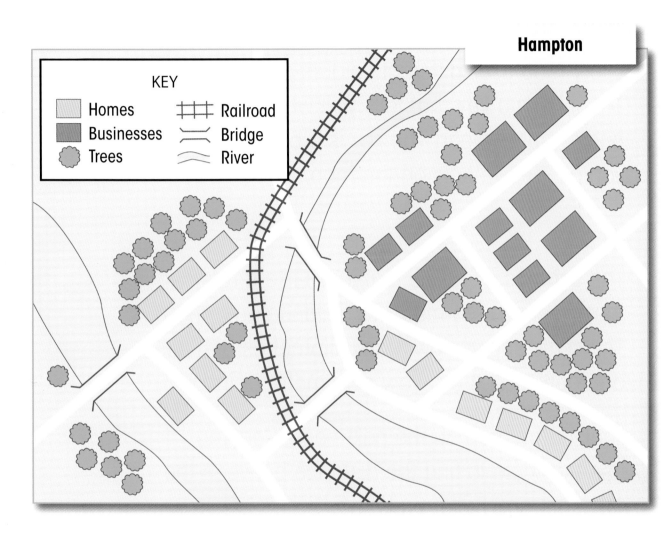

KEY

Homes

Businesses

Trees

Railroad

Bridge

River

Colour is often used as a symbol on maps. On the map above, blue shows a river. White lines show roads.

Map key

Every map uses different colours and **symbols**. Maps have a **key** that tells you what the colours and symbols mean. The key is a box that shows you all the symbols on the map.

Scale

The **scale** is a feature that looks like a ruler. It can help you to measure distance on a map. The scale shows how many kilometres or miles are represented by every centimetre or inch.

Look at the map on the next page. Can you use the scale to find the distance between the museum and Baker park?

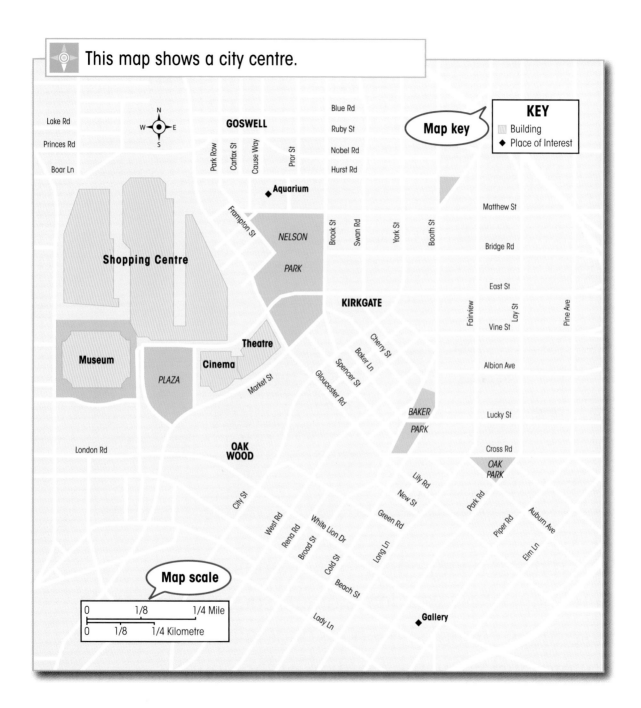

This map shows a city centre.

KEY
- Building
- ◆ Place of Interest

Map key

Map scale

Lake Rd
Princes Rd
Boar Ln

GOSWELL

Blue Rd
Ruby St
Nobel Rd
Hurst Rd

Park Row
Carfax St
Cause Way
Pror St

◆ Aquarium

Frampton St

NELSON

PARK

Brook St
Swan Rd
York St
Booth St

Matthew St
Bridge Rd
East St

Shopping Centre

KIRKGATE

Fairview
Vine St
Lay St
Pine Ave

Albion Ave

Cherry St
Baker Ln
Spencer St
Gloucester Rd

Theatre

Museum

Cinema

PLAZA

Market St

BAKER

PARK

Lucky St

Cross Rd

London Rd

OAK
WOOD

OAK
PARK

Park Rd

City St

Lily Rd
New St
Green Rd

Piper Rd
Auburn Ave

West Rd
Rena Rd
Broad St
White Lion Dr
Cold St
Beach St
Long Ln

Elm Ln

0   1/8   1/4 Mile
0   1/8   1/4 Kilometre

Lady Ln

◆ Gallery

13

Fitting things onto a map

Europe

ATLANTIC
OCEAN

Norwegian
Sea

NORWAY
SWEDEN
FINLAND
RUSSIA

ESTONIA

UNITED
KINGDOM

North
Sea

DENMARK

Baltic Sea

LATVIA

LITHUANIA

RUSSIA

IRELAND

NETHERLANDS

BELARUS

POLAND

BELGIUM
GERMANY

LUXEMBOURG

CZECH
REPUBLIC

UKRAINE

SLOVAKIA

FRANCE
SWITZERLAND
AUSTRIA
HUNGARY

MOLDOVA

SLOVENIA

ROMANIA

ANDORRA

CROATIA

SERBIA
AND
MONTENEGRO

PORTUGAL

ITALY

BOSNIA AND
HERZEGOVINA

Black Sea

SPAIN

BULGARIA

MACEDONIA

ALBANIA

Mediterranean

GREECE

TURKEY

A f r i c a

Sea

| 0 | 200 | 400 Miles |
| 0 | 200 | 400 Kilometres |

Maps must fit a large area onto a small surface.
Some maps show very large areas, such as **continents**.
These maps cannot show a lot of detail about a place.
They may just show the location of the country.

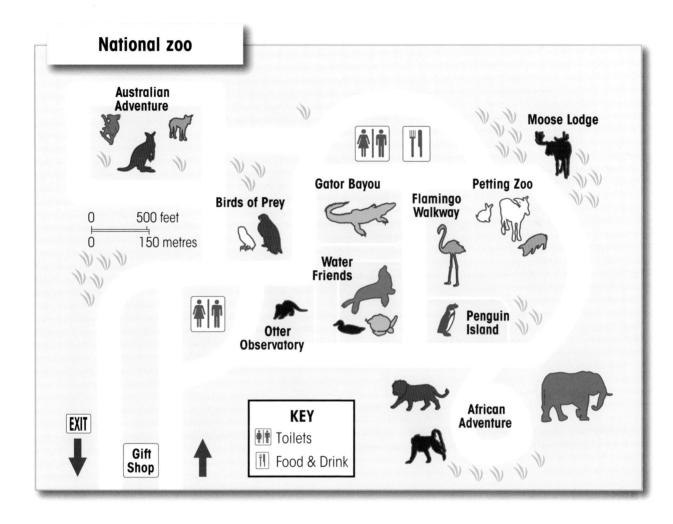

National zoo

Australian Adventure

Moose Lodge

Birds of Prey

0 — 500 feet
0 — 150 metres

Gator Bayou

Flamingo Walkway

Petting Zoo

Water Friends

Otter Observatory

Penguin Island

EXIT

Gift Shop

KEY

Toilets

Food & Drink

African Adventure

Other maps show smaller areas, such as cities or neighbourhoods. They may just show one place, such as a museum or zoo. These maps show more detail than country maps. They may show streets, parks, and important buildings in the area.

Mapping your classroom

A map can show a community as small as your classroom. Teachers often make maps of their classrooms called seating plans. A seating plan shows the teacher who sits where and helps the teacher to learn everyone's name.

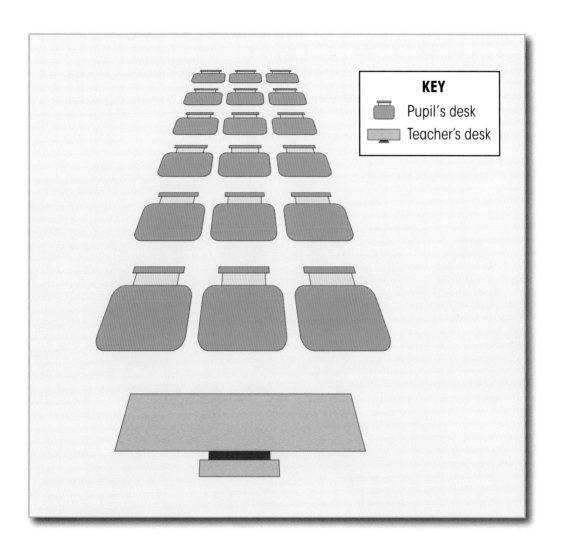

The map on this page shows a map of the classroom pictured on the left. It shows the location of each desk and shows where the teacher sits.

Mapping your school

A map can show a larger community, such as a school. A school is bigger than a classroom. This means a map of a school would show less detail than a map of a classroom.

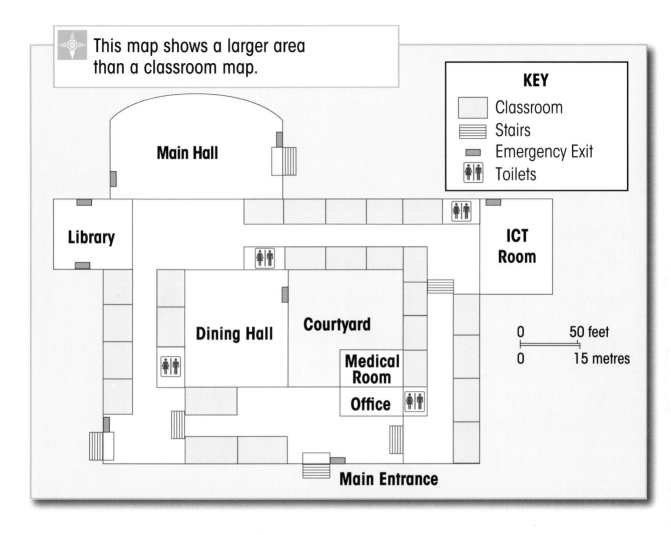

This map shows a larger area than a classroom map.

KEY
- Classroom
- Stairs
- Emergency Exit
- Toilets

Main Hall

Library

ICT Room

Dining Hall

Courtyard

Medical Room

Office

0   50 feet
0   15 metres

Main Entrance

A map of a school would show different information than a classroom map. The head teacher might use a school map to know the location of emergency exits and classrooms. The head teacher would not need a map with as much detail as a classroom map.

Mapping your neighbourhood

A neighbourhood includes the houses, flats, buildings, shops, parks, schools, and people in a small area.

A neighbourhood map shows the location of some of these places. This is important information for someone who wants to start a business, buy a house, or learn more about the area.

The map on the next page shows the different places in a neighbourhood. This map could be used to find the best way to travel from place to place. It shows a larger area than a map of a school, so the features are smaller.

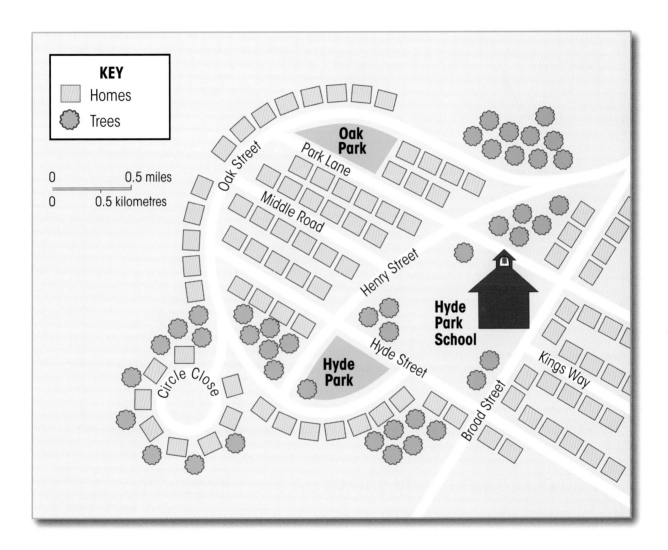

KEY
- Homes
- Trees

0 — 0.5 miles
0 — 0.5 kilometres

Oak Street
Park Lane
Oak Park
Middle Road
Henry Street
Hyde Park School
Hyde Street
Hyde Park
Circle Close
Broad Street
Kings Way

Mapping your town or city

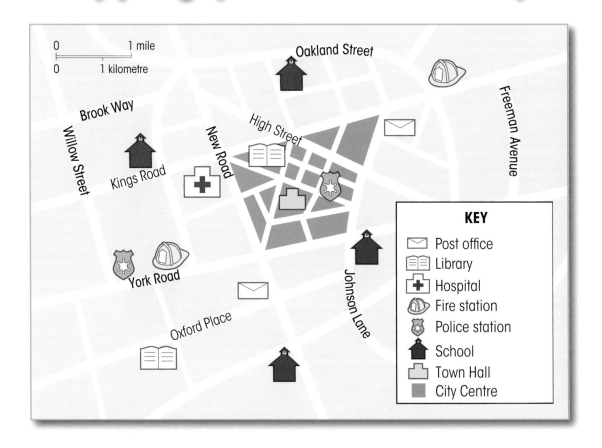

A map of a town or city shows an even larger area than a neighbourhood. It shows the location of important buildings, parks, and roads. The features on a town or city map are even smaller than the features on a neighbourhood map.

People who manage towns and cities need many maps. Firefighters need a map that shows the location of **hydrants**. If a pipe needs to be repaired, city workers need a map of the water pipes beneath the road.

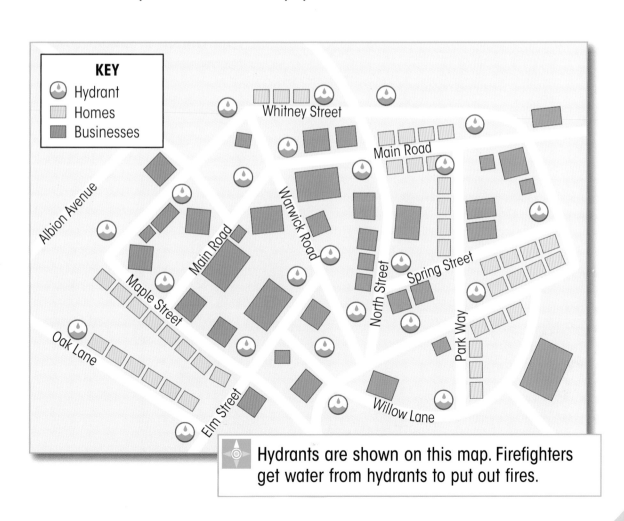

KEY
- Hydrant
- Homes
- Businesses

Whitney Street
Main Road
Albion Avenue
Warwick Road
Main Road
Maple Street
Oak Lane
North Street
Spring Street
Park Way
Elm Street
Willow Lane

Hydrants are shown on this map. Firefighters get water from hydrants to put out fires.

Mapping your country

Maps can show a very large community, such as a country. The map below shows the United Kingdom. The United Kingdom is made up of Scotland, England, Wales, and Northern Ireland.

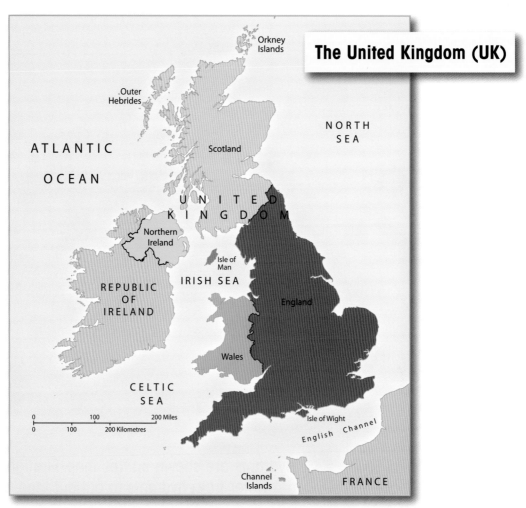

The United Kingdom (UK)

KEY

✪	Capital
★	Main city
●	Large city
•	City or town

A country map must fit an even larger area of land onto the map. It may only show a few major cities, the **capital** city, and large bodies of water.

How are maps made?

In order to make maps, people first need to collect the information for an area. Towns and cities hire people called **surveyors**. Surveyors carefully measure the location of roads, **hydrants**, and pipes in an area. They record the information to help **cartographers** to prepare a map.

Surveyors use special tools to measure the land.

Cartographers can create maps on computers.

Surveyors and cartographers can use photographs taken from an aeroplane to help them to make maps. Surveyors also use photographs taken by **satellites** from space.

Together, surveyors and cartographers map the communities around us. We use this information to learn more about places all over the world.

Map activities

Activity 1: Map your classroom

Imagine a new pupil is joining your class. Make a map of the classroom for this new pupil. You cannot show everything on your map, so think about what kind of information he or she will need to know. Don't forget to include features like a **title** and **key**.

Activity 2: Map your street

1. Think of a situation where someone would want a map of your street. Maybe a new family is moving to the street. Maybe the fire department would want a map in case there's a fire.

2. Make a list of the things your map will need to show.

3. Draw your map. Don't forget to include features like a title, **compass rose**, and key.

How would your map be different if it was of the whole neighbourhood?

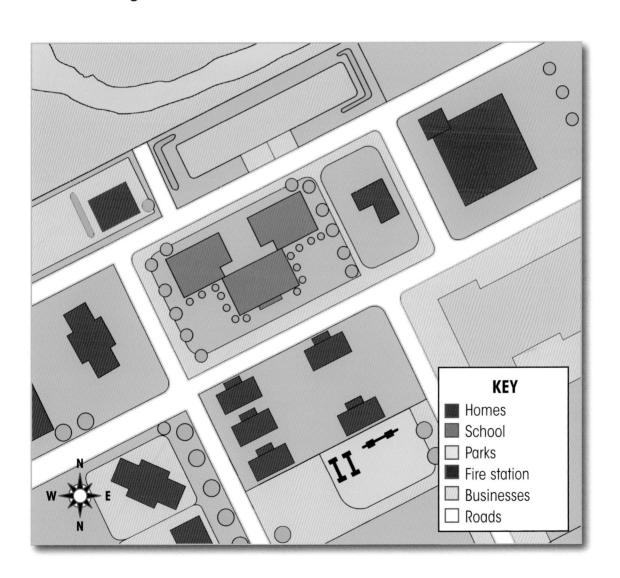

KEY
- Homes
- School
- Parks
- Fire station
- Businesses
- Roads

Glossary

captial city where leaders of a country meet and work

cardinal direction one of the four main directions: north, south, east, or west

cartographer person who makes maps

compass rose symbol on a map that shows direction

continent very large area of land surrounded by water; there are seven continents in the world.

hydrant water pipe in the ground that firefighters connect a hose to

key table that shows what the symbols on a map mean

satellite object that travels above the Earth and sends information back to the Earth

scale tool on a map that can be used to measure distance

surveyor person who makes measurements of the land

symbol picture that stands for something else

title feature that tells you what you will find on a map

Find out more

Organizations and websites

The websites below may have some advertisements on them. Ask an adult to look at them with you. You should never give out personal information, including your name and address, without talking to a trusted adult.

Google Maps
Visit Google maps (**maps.google.co.uk**) to find directions from your house to places nearby and far away. Try putting in your address and the address of your school. Do the directions given match your route?

National Geographic
National Geographic provides free maps and photos of the Earth. They also have articles about people and animals. Visit **www.nationalgeographic.com**.

Books to read

A Visit to: United Kingdom, Rachael Bell (Heinemann Library, 2008)

Heinemann First Atlas, Daniel Block and Marta Segal Block
     (Heinemann Library, 2007)

Inside Access: Maps & Mapping, Jinny Johnson and Lyn Store
     (Kingfisher, 2007)

Index